I.S.A.M. Monographs: Number 4

American Studies
and
American Musicology

A POINT OF VIEW AND A CASE IN POINT

RICHARD CRAWFORD

I.S.A.M. Monographs: Number 4

American Studies
and
American Musicology

A POINT OF VIEW AND A CASE IN POINT

RICHARD CRAWFORD

Institute for Studies in American Music
Department of Music
School of Performing Arts
Brooklyn College
of The City University of New York

Published by Institute for Studies in American Music,
Department of Music, School of Performing Arts,
Brooklyn College of the City University of New York
Brooklyn, New York 11210

INTRODUCTION

Under a grant from The Rockefeller Foundation, Richard Crawford was named Senior Research Fellow of the Institute for Studies in American Music for 1973-74. The two essays that follow were initially read as I.S.A.M. Fellowship Lectures—"American Studies and American Musicology" at the Graduate Center of the City University of New York, 4 March 1974, and "A Hardening of the Categories" at Brooklyn College, 14 March 1974. The lectures have been slightly revised by the author for publication.

Professor Crawford, Associate Professor in the School of Music of the University of Michigan, has been identified with American-music studies since completing a prize-winning dissertation, *Andrew Law: American Psalmodist,* which was awarded publication in the Pi Kappa Lambda Studies in American Music series. Other published articles, lectures, and ongoing research projects have established him as the foremost authority on early American psalmody in general. To be published shortly by Princeton University Press is his book (co-authored with David McKay), *William Billings: Eighteenth-Century American Composer.* Also approaching publication is his edition of *The Core Repertory of Early American Psalmody,* in the series Recent Researches in American Music (published by A-R Editions, Inc., under the editorial supervision of the Institute for Studies in American Music).

H. Wiley Hitchcock, Director
Institute for Studies in American Music
1 March 1975

CONTENTS

AMERICAN STUDIES AND AMERICAN MUSICOLOGY

The signs are plain that the study of American music is coming of age. The 1974 Winter Meetings of the Music Library Association in Champaign-Urbana can be taken as a symptom of this new condition. Afternoon sessions were devoted entirely to American music topics, and the evenings were given over to excellent performances of American music: a concert of new music, a jazz-band performance, a concert of gospel music, and a performance of the opera *Rip Van Winkle*, by the 19th-century American composer George Frederick Bristow. One meeting was devoted entirely to reports from various "centers" for the study of American music. Six different centers, including the Institute sponsoring this lecture, reported, and others could have been called upon. The American Musicological Society has U.S. Bicentennial plans which include an emphasis on American music unusual for the Society until very recent years. Government research agencies are inviting projects relating to the American Bicentennial. There is a marked increase in the proportion of graduate students intending to specialize in some aspect of American-music research. Journals not traditionally Americanist in perspective are, apparently as a matter of policy, printing articles on American music. Last year, the centennial of the birth of Oscar Sonneck, who set up the Music Division of the Library of Congress, and who was perhaps the first historian of music to take American music seriously, brought a flourish of Sonneck tributes, eulogies, evaluations—as if those interested in American music were looking to Sonneck for keys to the past, and hints for the future.

It is no secret that the study of American music has yet to claim much honor in the pantheon of American musicology. The basic reason is simple. Most American historians of music are so devoted to the music of Western Europe, and Western European music offers so many challenges and satisfactions to the intellect and musicianship and aesthetic sense, that there seems no good reason to study anything else. I might add that to many scholars American music, when compared with European, appears so much less worthy of attention, as music, that studying it seems a waste of time. Those who study American music know that it is not a waste of time, but they have not always found it easy to explain why. Ours, however, is an ecumenical age. For better or worse, sectarian differences are now unfashionable. This spirit has forced upon academics an ecumenicism—a tolerance for contrary propositions, a sense of obligation to hear them out—not unlike that of politicians. (In his book on Governor Earl Long of Louisiana, A. J. Liebling quotes one of the governor's campaign speeches which contains a ringing endorsement of ecumenicism. Governor Long claims to be the champion of black and white, Protestant, Catholic, and Jew, the rich, the poor, the middle-class—in fact, in Long's words, "just about everybody except Snake-Chunkers." Liebling explains: "The snake-chunkers, a small, fanatic cult, do not believe in voting.")[1] Even if academics, in their heart of hearts, have personal reservations about certain fields and their modes of inquiry, the fashion of the day is to hold the field innocent until proven guilty—to seem to take its legitimacy for granted, while waiting for the expected stumbles and signs of weakness. American music is now having its chance in the musicological arena. It would be an exaggeration to claim that, as the field of American studies begins its perilous journey across the tightrope, musicology, tense and expectant, watches and waits. Yet this is a propitious moment for scholars of American music to demonstrate their wares. Just what are these wares? Is there a particular style of American musicology, as reflected in American studies? If so, how can it be described, and what can be learned from it?

One way to gauge the temper of an academic field is to examine its monuments. My own list of American musicological monuments—of indispensable works about American music that affect our whole outlook, that we consult every day or once did—would include Sonneck's *Early Concert-Life in America*, Sonneck-Upton's *Bibliography of Early Secular American Music*, Richard Wolfe's *Secular Music in America 1801-1825*, Irving Lowens's *Music and Musicians in Early America*, John Kirkpatrick's "Temporary Mimeographed Catalogue of the Music Manuscripts and related materials of Charles Edward Ives," and Gilbert Chase's *America's Music*. The legacy of these monuments is various. From Sonneck and Wolfe we get an exhaustive description of non-sacred music published in America through 1825. We also get a notion that any musical repertory, no matter what its aesthetic value may seem to be, has its own story to tell, its own secrets to reveal.

Lowens and Kirkpatrick provide models of how sympathy and a respect for detail can illuminate. Lowens's studies of 18th- and early 19th-century psalmody, especially in its bibliographical aspects, light some of the most unpromising corners of past American musical experience. Kirkpatrick's scrupulous respect for materials of all kinds relating to Ives provides an approach to the music and musical thought of a great composer. Chase offers a perspective in which American music is shown to have values different from, rather than inferior to, European music—values in which the center of gravity is found in popular rather than in so-called serious musical forms. (It should be noticed in passing that none of these "monuments" was produced by a Ph.D. in musicology.)

The legacy of these monuments is fragmentary indeed when compared with the monuments that European music studies have produced. Missing are the major touchstones of traditional musical scholarship: the rows of collected works in folio volumes, the monumental biographies, the genre studies, and the period studies. The present-day scholar of European music, by courtesy of tradition, begins with a value-system, an archive of precious and not-so-precious objects (many ready to use), and bibliographical and biographical maps which distinguish well-worn paths, underdeveloped terrain, and *terra incognita*. By contrast, the scholar of American music has no established value-system (even his monuments sometimes speak in riddles), his archive is a kind of junkheap—the gems are buried in a rubble of sheet-music, newspaper clippings, song collections, manuscripts by unknowns —and the best maps are of the other side of the tracks. (*Is* there a more prosperous section of town?) What the scholar of American music is left with, then, is a huge mass of music and information—mostly unassimilated, a few excellent tools for handling it, and a belief which he hopes is not an illusion. Henry James put the belief this way:

> To be at all critically . . . minded . . . is to be subject to the superstition that objects and places, coherently grouped, disposed for human use and addressed to it, must have a sense of their own, a mystic meaning proper to themselves to give out: to give out, that is, to the participant at once so interested and so detached as to be moved to a report of the matter.[2]

As we mentioned some "monuments" of scholarship in American music, we left present-day American musical scholarship as she was beginning her walk over the Bicentennial tightrope. There really should be no fear of a fall. If studies in American music were merely a timely patriotic gesture or a belated bow toward an unjustly neglected field, 1977, the post-Bicentennial year, might indeed see the bubble burst. I believe, however, that the legacy of American studies and its peculiar situation within the field of American musicology has led it to establish its own profile; that the special concerns and approaches it has developed differ from those of the scholar of European music; and even that American scholars of European music stand to learn from the Americanist perspective. American topics may be currently popular because of the Bicentennial. Yet that popularity is no pseudo-event: it signals a qualitative change in progress, a change that will affect American musicology as a whole.

What particular traits determine the profile of American musical studies? First, the scholar of American music assumes significance, does not claim musical value as a prior condition; second, whether by instinct or training, he tries to take each piece of music on its own terms; third, he recognizes the importance of keeping his musical responses open on many levels, striving for inclusive rather than selective perception; fourth, he tries at all times to keep in mind his position as a participant in the musical culture he is studying. These precepts are obviously interrelated, and perhaps only the fourth can be claimed as peculiar to American studies. All need further comment.

The scholar of American music is not indifferent to value. But he learns that there are values other than aesthetic value, and he also learns the hazards of judging value quickly—especially when the genre is modest or the style unusual. The second tenet, taking each piece on its own terms, is obviously a basic tenet of ethnomusicology. A major task in both ethnomusicology and American-music studies is to answer this question: according to what terms is this piece or this genre comprehensible or meaningful? The third proposition—a corollary to the second, that one must respond to many different kinds of music, each on its own level—is built into the experience of most students of American music. Most have grown up with, been trained in, and have a deep and continuing love for "great" European music. By choosing, at the same time, to study aspects of American music that may have little or nothing to do with European mainstreams, the historian of American music divides himself among sharply varying repertories. His thoughts, therefore, tend to run along comparative lines. He seeks out conjunctions and interfaces between repertories. He is likely to give far more attention to co-ordinating and reflecting upon his musical responses than his more single-minded colleague. The fourth proposition—in James's phrase, the historian as the "participant at once so interested and so detached as to be moved to a report of the matter"—has weighty implications which I will take up later.

In case these four propositions do not immediately suggest how the climate of American-music studies might come to alter American musicology as a whole, I might point out that they run essentially counter to traditional musicological tenets. The scholar of European music, having inherited a standard of value, takes his stand with the music of the Great Masters. He need not take each piece on its own terms, since he already has a perfectly good set of terms to take pieces on: the values established by the Masters and the mainstream in which they worked. (Of course scholars of European music have had to confront unusual and unfamiliar music in their training, and as musicology has penetrated beyond the ranks of the Great Masters it has become more hesitant to dismiss works peremptorily. However, both the unfamiliar and the possibly mediocre are still viewed as part of the European mainstream, and with some effort both can be seen to partake of its glimmer, however dimly.) On the third point: a scholar of European music may keep his hand in several repertories—perhaps for recreation or extra income—but seldom do they engage his serious attention. Finally, most American scholarship on European music is written from a position of objective, "professional" detachment. The writer has no illusions of his own involvement in any essential aspect of the music, so he treats it respectfully, as a separate, venerated object.

These differences in outlook are reflected in the views that scholars of European music and scholars of American music inherit of their respective traditions. Both the living performance tradition in "serious" music and the inherited academic tradition conspire to depict the history of European music as a closed, unified, almost monolithic system. Individual historians, of course, with experience, fight clear of this notion but it is very powerful. Books, articles, recordings, concerts in great number seem to ratify the great mainstream of Western European music as a single inevitable evolutionary process; it becomes difficult to get far enough from it to see it as anything else, or to see anything else as important next to it. Only from a distance is one likely to see Western European music as an assortment of very different things. The unity it may seem to possess up close looks from this distance imposed rather than inherent. Furthermore, the perspective of distance discloses other streams, some related to the European, some not. Scholars of American music are bequeathed quite a different view. Only in popular and ethnic musics, and in contemporary music, do they inherit living performance traditions. The received academic tradition, through its relative silence, suggests the probable inferiority of American music, or at least its irrelevance and demonstrable difference from European music. Thus, students of American music who look beyond the present find their slate more or less clean. The scholar of European music is presented with something like a *fait accompli,* or at least an image in which most of the "reality" is already determined. He must rationalize it, much as a geologist might explain how the topography of a certain region came to be. The scholar of American music looks out over a flat landscape, and he fills it in. He has to discover facts and plant them where now nothing stands. Once he learns what is out there, he has to determine what is important and what isn't. Since it is left to him to fabricate history, he presumably learns what history is, how fragile a tissue of fact and inference. He learns what it can tell us and what it cannot. In short, the writer of American musical history is forced to begin outside his subject, and he must consciously locate himself and his narrative in some newly-built structure of fact. In contrast, once the historian of European music assumes his value-system, he can work indoors. He can begin well within his subject, can trope well-known historical precepts, can add facts and interpretations and reinterpretations to the narrative, can end up with full confidence that his topic is important and that he has dealt with it properly. It may not occur to him that he occupies a space-ship, not a planet. This is by no means to suggest that the Americanist writes better history or makes more valuable contributions. It is just that he is obliged to be conscious of the place of his work in the larger scheme of things, of its arbitrariness and tentativeness, in a way that his colleague may not be. The Americanist has learned not to take anything for granted.

Another difference in the tenor and tone of European-music studies as opposed to American is influenced by a powerful force in American life. The characteristic American metaphor is upward mobility. Upward mobility is a recurrent motif in education, in business, in literature, in politics, and elsewhere. In the arts, this tendency has been felt in the desire to improve taste. The ladder, or some other kind of down-to-up conveyance, is a simile frequently invoked in polemics on musical taste. For example, the 19th-century American song composer, George Frederick Root, saw himself as an agent in the battle to improve the taste of his countrymen. In his autobiography, *Story of a Musical Life*, Root admitted in so many words that he was no Schubert. His songs were written, he explained, to serve as a kind of middle of the ladder. He hoped that they would help his countrymen rise above the musical debasement of their early lives, and perhaps even stimulate some to scale Schubertian heights.[3] Writing on American music education, Allen Britton has observed:

> Politeness is what Americans have wanted from their schools. . . . American families, generally speaking, have sent their children to school hoping to open a better way of life for them; not, in other words, to train them for an accepted way of life, but to prepare them for entrance into the life of the next higher social class. . . . An education in music has always been considered somehow to be genteel, and the prospect of being able to follow a musical career has, traditionally for most Americans, seemed to represent a decided social and cultural advancement.[4]

As Britton suggests, and as things have worked out in music, the unspoken goal of this educational process has been not so much to widen musical taste as to upgrade it: to replace a taste for one kind of music with a taste for another, better kind. Britton is writing here about public school education, but much of what he says applies to the education of music historians. Musicological education is primarily a training in selective perception. It concentrates on depth and penetration at the expense of breadth and coordination. It says no to many things in the belief that its ringing yes to one will inspire "professional" results. To plunge into the study of ancient and arcane musics, to submit to the scholar's yoke and to enter a world of bibliography, watermarks, call-numbers—a world with a value-system so remote from one's daily life—is surely to alter one's status or social class, if not monetarily at least psychologically. One's musical taste is also likely to change. There is a strong tendency during the professional education of a musicologist for what H. Wiley Hitchcock has called the "vernacular"—music which one has "grown into" naturally without effort or self-consciousness—to be replaced by the "cultivated"—music consciously sought after and studied for the spiritual edification it offers.[5] This is the musicological equivalent of upward mobility. It is hard for the student of European music not to move "up" to a musical world more genteel, more consistent, more controllable than the one he inherits. It is essential for the student of American music *not* to make such a move. He must learn his trade while resisting the transformation that often goes with it. It is his business to retain a sense of where the boundaries between vernacular and cultivated lie, to keep his reflexes sharp and his taste limber.

This brings us to the question of the individual historian as a member of a culture, as a participant in its musical life. In *The Past Recaptured*, the last volume of *Remembrance of Things Past*, Marcel Proust writes of the artistic insights that came to him when, after years of isolation, he went out again into society. Thinking himself a failed, sterile writer, Proust experienced in society flashes of insight which signalled to him that all of the material he would ever need to write about was lodged in his own memory. One comment in particular is relevant to our discussion. It is, in fact, the basic text for the rest of this lecture. Proust here evaluates the relative significance of what we are here calling vernacular and cultivated experience. He writes:

> The truths which the intellect apprehends directly in the world of full and unimpeded light have something less profound, less necessary then those which life communicates to us against our will in an impression which is material because it enters us through the senses but yet has a spiritual meaning which it is possible for us to extract.[6]

Proust is speaking here as a creative artist, but I believe that his comment applies to historians, and especially to historians of music. (That the historian's vocation is artistic as well as scholarly is a familiar enough notion not to need defense here.) Proust distinguishes between value in the quality of experience and value in the object producing the experience. He finds the quality of experience more significant than the value of the object causing it. (C.S. Lewis's *An Experiment in Criticism*, a small and enlightening book, is written to support that very point.) Moreover, Proust insists that vernacular experience, far from being haphazard or casual, is rigorous. With phrases such as "dictated to us" and "austere school of life," he describes experience "communicated to us against our will." Unsought, vernacular experience in this view becomes "necessary;" cultivated experience becomes supplementary. Proust's view challenges the individual to come to grips with experience that "is material because it enters us through the senses." As sense experience, it is lodged in us, together with other such experiences, as if in thousands of sealed vessels. These experiences preserve a "spiritual meaning which it is possible for us to extract." That last phrase is fair warning. Extracting this experience, Proust tells us, is a cruel task. His own image of the process pictures a diver groping for and stumbling against and following the contours of the ocean floor. Vernacular experience lodged in the sense memory is specific, not general. It is fact, not concept; concrete, not abstract. "Dictated by reality," it cannot be summoned by reason, cannot be forged or simulated, only rediscovered and captured by a disciplined and lucky intellect. "The inner book of unknown symbols," as Proust calls involuntary sense experience, is the hardest book of all to read and the most valuable.

Historians of music deal with both sense experience and intellectual experience, and they are sometimes confused about just how to do it. Virtually all musicologists are practicing musicians, or were at some time. Before that they were players, listeners, whistlers, singers. Had their own vernacular background not been intense, they would hardly have chosen music as a profession. Like most musicians, historians are born with some special aural aptitude, and they have worked to train this faculty. Moreover, they are not satisfied to remain ignorant of the structure, techniques, and general workings of the music they admire. They submit the evidence of their disciplined ears and memories to the disciplined inquiry of their minds. This is standard musicological procedure. So far, so good. However, the only music that musicologists are likely to scrutinize closely is music brought forward by conscious decision—music, in Proust's phrase, "which the intellect apprehends directly in the world of full and unimpeded light." What about music "communicated to us against our will"? What about our own musical vernacular— the musical baggage we carry around with us but never give much attention to: scraps of operas and quartets, alma maters, hymns, nursery rhymes, commercials, pop-tunes from our past? Proust's statement suggests that these are not merely random leavings. He suggests that powerful sense impulses chose them—impulses almost surely now forgotten— and he also implies that we will be enlightened if we can discover what these impulses were, and why our senses chose certain pieces and not others "against our will." Every music historian has his own professional "cultivated" repertories; every music historian also has his own "inner book of unknown symbols": his own internal musical vernacular.

Proust's insistence on the rigor and necessity of vernacular experience supports the intuition of the student of American music. The "vernacular" and "cultivated" streams in his own life, however, are not always easy to separate or identify. Vernacular experience is constantly accumulating; it does not belong exclusively to the past. Yet an academic finds it difficult to have distinctively vernacular experiences—experiences that are deeply felt and not analyzed as they are going on. He develops a kind of alert-mechanism that swings into operation almost involuntarily, converting vernacular experience into cultivated on the spot, forcing the experience to unfold in "the world of full and unimpeded light." (As if in recognition of this fact, when Studs Terkel interviewed Chicagoans of almost all descriptions about their lives, and used these interviews as the basis for his book, *Division Street*, he chose not to include professors among his subjects.) Proust has a statement which helps to explain, and not sentimentally, why a plain layman's vernacular experience is likely to mean more than a trained professional's, and why a professional's preprofessional experience is likely to be more rigorously vernacular than his later experience. He says: "There is a closer analogy between the instinctive life of the public and the talent of a great writer . . . than between this same talent and the superficial verbiage and changing criteria of the established judges of literature." And what does Proust find in both the common man's and great writer's approach to experience that is missing from the academic's? "Simply an instinct religiously listened to in the midst of a silence imposed upon all other voices."[7] The academic works to develop his questioning, cultivated, second voice, but then he finds it very difficult to shut it up, even when its restless probing distracts him in moments when he might find himself listening "religiously" to "an instinct . . . in the midst of a silence imposed upon all other voices." Another difficulty with the supposed vernacular-cultivated dichotomy is that historians of music have lived so long and so closely with "their" repertories that they make essentially vernacular responses to what were once cultivated objects. Music originally cultivated turns into a kind of vernacular for them. But it is never their *only* vernacular; there was already another vernacular there before it.

To recognize vernacular experience as essential and ongoing rather than replaceable and perishable is to accept the premise that the historian needs to pay attention to many kinds of music: it ratifies the importance of multiple levels of musical experience. Multiple levels have already been mentioned as a fact of life for the historian of American music. And his recognition of it should make it easier for him to cope with present-day musical life in the United States. The basic facts of present musical life are its multiplicity and availability. By virtue of editions, performing groups, and recordings, the music of the Western world since the Middle Ages is unrolled before our very eyes and ears—or at least a massive chunk of it is. We can also become connoisseurs of ethnic musics from almost anywhere on the globe. In addition, the so-called popular music industry each week issues a torrent of new products; currently, under the tag "nostalgia," it also makes available pop music of the past. Thus, the diversity of music available, and the chronological variety of each type, make America today a musical consumer's paradise. Obviously, no single person can command this whole range; but neither can we be sure that anyone can escape its effects. We have learned, in this ecologically-minded age, that disparate phenomena are often interrelated.[8] Therefore, it becomes hard to believe that the enormous diversity and ubiquitousness of music—phenomena new to our age—have no real influence on our perception of any single repertory. The student of American music, with his supposedly sharp, multiple-level reflexes, will be thrown into a Saint Vitus's dance of accommodation if he tries to co-ordinate his responses to all this music. But if we concede that the topic is not trivial, his is the kind of sensibility best suited to deal with it.

The word "nostalgia" has come up, and the changing meaning of the word is pertinent to this discussion. As used by the entertainment industry and by journalism, it refers to the resurrection of discarded artifacts of the past—usually harmless. Popular culture is the chief source for this class of objects collectively referred to as nostalgia. Nostalgia also refers to the emotion one is supposed to feel when confronted by such objects. The word has come to connote something quite close to sentimentality—a kind of gentle wish for the days to which the resurrected objects belonged, and, as a corollary, a vague but distinct impression that those days were better days, more innocent, really better suited to the wisher's sensibilities than the coarser, more brutal realities of the present. The *American Heritage Dictionary* supports this meaning of nostalgia, giving as its first definition "a longing for things, persons, or situations that are not present." If we grant that the longing need not be intense, this definition opens the door of nostalgia to all comers. Since there may or may not be a prior link between the consumer and the "things, persons, or situations that are not present," nostalgia could run the gamut from a widower's grieving for his wife to a teenager's response to a tape of the *Vic and Sade* radio program, which went off the air around 1950. Not a very precise term. The second meaning of nostalgia in the *American Heritage Dictionary* is the only meaning in the *Oxford English Dictionary* of 1933. Quoting from the *O.E.D.*, nostalgia is "a form of melancholia caused by prolonged absence from one's home or country; severe home-sickness"—nothing gentle or harmless about that. Without launching a diatribe about the denaturing of this word, and without seeming to attach too much significance to it, I think it is fair to call the change decadent. It severs the original organic connection between a deep feeling and its cause, it denies the specificity and hence the importance of a particular emotion, and, by doing both, it implies that a longing is a longing is a longing. The peculiar, powerful, necessary quality of nostalgia in its original sense is loosened and diffused. When I say "necessary quality," I am, of course, trying to steer the train of thought back toward Proust and his affirmation that vernacular experience is essential experience. Nostalgia in its original meaning is involuntary, instinctive, and vernacular. What is now peddled as nostalgia is really a voluntary conjunction of memory and imagination. The importance of nostalgia as an artistic force as well as a historical stimulus is clear enough in American music. In fact, precisely because we do *not* think of Charles Ives as a gentle figure, it is well to recall that his music is rooted in nostalgic experience. Recognizing that Ives returned again and again to boyhood experiences for musical inspiration should help us to remember that nostalgia can encompass fierceness as well as reverie. Ives struggled to read the "inner book of unknown symbols." He kept his vernacular life alive, and he succeeded in extracting the "spiritual meaning" from experience communicated "against his will;" he "submitted" to the "reality" lodged in his memory. Ives is the American composer corresponding most closely with Proust's idea of how an artist pursues his vocation. With that in mind, we can hardly afford to condescend to nostalgia as a force.

The historian of American music, with his recognition of the incontrovertibility of his own vernacular, can also remind his colleagues of the importance of musical taste as an issue and of its mysterious working as a force. Taste—in Hannah Arendt's description, "the discriminating, discerning, judging elements of an active love of beauty"[9]—has been the center of an ideological issue of great importance in American musical life since the 18th century. The art music to which primary value has been attached was originally an American importation, not a native growth. American advocates of art music from the beginning tended to hover around its fragile stalk, anxiously trying to coax out blooms and exhorting the public at large to exhibit "good taste" by loving it as they professed to do. In a society like ours, where education has invited repudiation of past experience and status, the arts have sometimes served as emblems of the upwardly mobile. The cry for "good taste" in art has sometimes been taken up as a social, rather than an artistic, cause. How "good taste" as an ideal has been digested by the Philistine mentality is a most interesting story, but it is a side issue here. Our question concerns the development of individual taste—specifically the personal musical taste of music historians. Some time ago we briefly mentioned the professional musician's personal—presumably upward—odyssey through vernacular to cultivated. What marked the path for each of us? What did we learn on the journey? What did we bring with us? What did we leave behind? Why? What do we really know about our individual taste and the forces that shaped it?

Taste is a mysterious and underinvestigated property. We usually say "It's a matter of taste" to end a debate, meaning that there's no point discussing an idiosyncrasy further. Taste is thought to be a phenomenon so personal that attempts to rationalize or explain it could hardly be of any use to anyone else. We like what we like, hate what we hate, and why can't it be left at that? The historian cannot afford to leave it at that, because his taste is the key to his "inner book of unknown symbols." Music which once had for him the richest significance, gave the deepest satisfactions, mysteriously loses its appeal. On the other hand, his taste forces upon him a set of responses in which, for example, an alma mater, a televised insurance commercial, and a particular passage from Schumann's piano concerto occupy equal status, all capable of dissolving him into a helpless state of emotional and musical acquiescense—even though the three pieces are given wildly different values by his intellect. The slightest scrutiny of one's taste reveals such changes and gaps. Their apparent inconsistency and haphazardness, their unwillingness to yield up easy explanations, may lead us to overlook the whole realm—to let it remain a kind of unconscious undercurrent. If, indeed, the historian of music sets aside his vernacular experience and allows his mind to dictate his value-system, he can avoid messy contradictions. But if he takes the intensity and quality of his vernacular experience as a touchstone, and if he is willing to live with contradictions, he has in his grasp a historical tool of great power. Concentrating on his own involuntary responses and their unpredictability—nonexistent when they should be strong; overwhelming, sometimes, when they should be weak—he can begin to try to read his own "inner book of unknown symbols."

Proust describes the writer working from that book, seeking above all to connect what has become separated:

> Truth will be attained by him only when he takes two different objects [and] states the connection between them . . . truth—and life too—can be attained by us only when, by comparing a quality common to two sensations, we succeed in extracting their common essence and in reuniting them to each other, liberated from the contingencies of time, within a metaphor.[10]

This description helps us to see taste and experience as sources rather than emblems, as deposits in which contradictory impressions and attitudes, both vernacular and cultivated, co-exist. Transferred to the musical realm, it invites music historians to try to understand their instinctive taste in order to understand more about the nature of music and the function of different kinds of music in different cultures—including European and including their own. A healthy taste is muddled and opaque, but its surprises and richness are near-inexhaustible. To try to understand one's taste is to court frustration; to fail to try to understand it is to accept a handicap.

Every historian of music has undergone a process of education, and this process has in some way affected his vernacular. The precise nature of the effect will be different for each individual. And partly for that reason, the working of that process in each individual is unique. I am not suggesting that musicologists write autobiographies. I am, however, suggesting that there is probably nothing in a historian's life more important to his vocation than the changes which he experiences in his education and the way he deals with these changes. In a book called *The Country and the City* Raymond Williams notes the importance of the writer's developing an educated consciousness of the facts of change.[11] Each historian of music commands materials that can lead him precisely to that educated consciousness of the facts of change—his own experience as a receiver of music.

When one examines himself as a receiver and participant, he naturally becomes interested in the way other people receive music, or have received it in the past. This leads to interest in forgotten repertories, where all that remains is lots of apparently worthless music and evidence that people once liked it. If the interest is real, it will lead to study of the music, and if study then leads to performance, a new set of realities and changes is set in motion. So long as a negative historical reputation of a piece or repertory forestalls performance, the reputation is safe. When a piece or a repertory, however, is brought to life in performance, when it can be heard and seen as well as studied, it is liberated, at least momentarily, from that historical judgment and allowed to exist once again on the sense level. And for the historian, whether the result eventually confirms the original judgment or denies it, that piece and repertory can never be quite the same again. To take an example: those who have heard the University of Illinois's American Music Group perform 19th-century American music, or who have heard their recordings, or who know the album of 19th-century popular concert and parlor music in America recorded by their leader, Neely Bruce, may have had reactions similar to my own—equivocal and even queasy initial feelings about the legitimacy of the venture; uproarious, almost crippling bouts of laughter; a sense of being unexpectedly moved at times by the sincerity of the music and the integrity of the performers; finally, an altered notion of what constitutes a musical cliché, or at least new doubt that clichés are to be avoided at all costs. When one finds satisfying musical moments in so lowly and clichéd and convention-ridden a repertory, one is forced to reconsider the function of clichés and conventions in "great" music. Encounters with unfamiliar, even discredited, repertories are apt to be disturbing.

Modern musical scholarship as practiced in America, for all of its many and obvious virtues, has tended to view itself rather narrowly. Perhaps partly in reaction to earlier, anecdotal "history" and facile, free-associative descriptions of music set forth as "analysis," musicology has embraced a "scientific," "objective" credo. From this perspective the historian is inclined in his professional capacity to suspect and mistrust anything with a whiff of the personal or the subjective about it. His own early vernacular experience, his instinctive taste and its evolution, the music which causes him nostalgia, his involuntary sensibility as a whole may seem to him a kind of mysterious, sometimes distracting baggage he would just as soon discard. He is inclined to treat this personal realm, in fact (if he treats it at all), as something entirely separate from his "real" life, i.e. his life and work as a professional scholar of music. It may seem to him vague and unfocused in a way that professional experience—carried on "in the world of full and unimpeded light"—never is. Proust tells us that this is an illusion. He reminds us that the artist/writer/historian is a participant in the culture he studies, that he cannot remove himself from it, and that, moreover, his experience as a participant is precisely what imparts a rigor and a reality and a necessity to his observations. Nor does this emphasis on individual taste and personal vernacular experience necessarily lead to narcissim. The historian is enjoined not to gaze raptly at his own reflection but to accept the Socratic injunction against living an unexamined life; he is urged to seek musical self-knowledge.

The historian of American music has had to define necessity differently from his colleagues who study European music. Their necessity has been essentially external and aesthetic; his is internal and emotional. They deal primarily with the objects—with, as the saying goes, the music itself, though I have never understood quite why we have to say "itself." He may deal with the objects too, but he also is concerned with the reception of the objects and with relationships between different kinds of objects. These lines of inquiry keep him in motion, conscious of his dual role as participant and observer, occupied with comparisons on many levels, looking for hidden and unsuspected links. He is unified, in effect, chiefly by his trust in his own sensibility, however murky that sensibility may be.

Proust tells us that when the "inner book of unknown symbols" is read, when two different objects are "reunited," they are "liberated from the contingencies of time." The past rushes into the present, and past and present are fused outside the dimension of time. When training and experience lead to an "educated consciousness of the facts of change," when they require a widening of the horizons rather than a novitiate's vow to renounce his past, the historian's whole experience accompanies him in his investigations of both past and present. Thus, the student of American music has chosen a field which, however unpromising it may seem to an outsider, accepts him whole, urges him to remain whole, and leads him to study American musical culture from the perspective of wholeness. He invites American musicology as a whole to heed that example.

NOTES

1. A. J. Liebling, *The Earl of Louisiana* (New York: Simon and Schuster, 1961), pp. 91, 93.

2. Attributed to James, *The American Scene*, in Wright Morris, *The Home Place* (Bison paperback ed., Lincoln: University of Nebraska Press, 1968), where it appears as the introductory quotation.

3. George F. Root, *The Story of a Musical Life* (Cincinnati: John Church Co., 1891), pp. 19-20.

4. Allen P. Britton, "Music Education: An American Specialty," in Paul Henry Lang, ed., *One Hundred Years of Music in America* (New York: G. Schirmer, 1961), p. 215.

5. H. Wiley Hitchcock, *Music in the United States*, 2nd ed. (Englewood Cliffs: Prentice-Hall, 1974), p. 51.

6. Marcel Proust, *The Past Recaptured*, trans. Andreas Mayor (Vintage paperback ed., New York, 1971), p. 138.

7. Proust, *The Past Recaptured*, p. 150.

8. An interesting commentary on changing attitudes toward the relatedness of religious and political problems appears in Garry Wills, *Bare Ruined Choirs: Doubt, Prophecy, and Radical Religion* (Garden City: Doubleday, 1972), Chapter 4, especially p. 90.

9. Hannah Arendt, *Between Past and Future: Six exercises in Political Thought* (Meridian paperback ed., Cleveland and New York, 1963), p. 219.

10. Proust, *The Past Recaptured*, p. 147.

11. Raymond Williams, *The Country and the City* (New York: Oxford University Press, 1973). See especially Chapters 18, 22, and 25 (i).

A HARDENING OF THE CATEGORIES: "VERNACULAR," "CULTIVATED," AND REACTIONARY IN AMERICAN PSALMODY

In December 1770 there was published in Boston a large collection of sacred music composed by William Billings, a 24-year-old local tanner and musician. The collection carried an unmistakable made-in-America stamp, distinguishing it from earlier American tune-books—with its title (*The New-England Psalm-Singer; or, American Chorister*) and authorship, its frontispiece engraved by the local silversmith, Paul Revere, its prefatory poems by the Rev. Mather Byles, pastor of Boston's Hollis Street Congregational Church, its inclusion of hymn texts by New Englanders as well as the inevitable Tate and Brady and Dr. Watts, and its adoption of the names of Massachusetts counties and towns and Boston streets and churches as tune titles. The introduction to Billings's work was hardly less remarkable than its music. It included a long and somewhat scientific "Essay on the Nature and Properties of Sound" (not by Billings), an extensive set of instructions on the rudiments and workings of music, two poems by Mather Byles, and several personal statements by the author. Billings is such a compelling writer that it is always hard to quote him briefly. But I will restrain myself here and quote only three passages which bear directly on the topic at hand. In the first Billings describes his credentials as a composer.

> Altho' this Composition hath cost me much Time and Pains; yet I little thought of exposing it to public View; But being repeatedly importuned by my Friends, I was at last prevailed upon to commit it to the Press. And such as it is I now offer it to the Public. . . . Perhaps there may appear in the Eyes of the Accurate much Incorrectness that I was not able to discern; therefore would beg the Critic to be tender, and rectify those Errors which through Inexperience may happen to have escaped the Notice of a Youth, in the Course of so large a Volume. (p.2)

The second, much briefer, deals with the character or style of the music in the collection:

> In the Composition I have been as plain and simple as possible; and yet have tried to the utmost of my Power to preserve the modern Air and Manner of Singing. (p.2)

The third, surely the most resonant and best-known statement by any 18th-century American musician, is a bold assertion of creative independence. It symbolizes the birth of a new American attitude toward composing music. I am less concerned, however, with that aspect of Billings's statement than with something else to be noted in it: the issue of musical idiom or grammar.

> Perhaps it may be expected by some, that I should say something concerning Rules for Composition; to these I answer that *Nature* is the best Dictator, for all the hard dry studied Rules that ever was prescribed, will not enable any person to form an Air any more than the bare Knowledge of the four and twenty letters, and strict Grammatical Rules will qualify a Scholar for composing a Piece of Poetry, or properly adjusting a Tragedy, without a Genius. It must be Nature, Nature must lay the Foundation, Nature must inspire the Thought. But perhaps some may think I mean and intend to throw Art intirely out of the Question. I answer by no Means, for the more Art is display'd, the more Nature is decorated. . . . I have read several Author's Rules on Composition, and find the strictest of them make some Exceptions, as thus, they say that two Eighths or two Fifths may not be taken together rising or falling, unless one be Major and the other Minor; but rather than spoil the Air, they will allow that Breach to be made, and this allowance gives great Latitude to young Composers, for they may always make that Plea, and say, if I am not allow'd to transgress the Rules of Composition, I shall certainly spoil the Air, and Cross the Strain, that fancy dictated. (p.19)

The three interrelated themes Billings touches upon here—the American as a composer, the style of music appropriate for sacred use, and the idiom of sacred music—were to be major ideological points as American sacred music developed in the late 18th and early 19th century. It is the purpose of this paper to trace the development of ideas on these three topics and to comment on the issues they raise.

The idea of the American as a composer was born rather slowly. James Lyon's *Urania* (Philadelphia, 1761) is the first colonial collection to distinguish the provenance of its music in any way.[1] Lyon identifies six pieces as "never before published," hence as American compositions. Prior to that time several tunes apparently composed by Americans had appeared in the colonies, but the compilers who printed them did not identify them as native products. American psalmody before Lyon had restricted itself to a relatively small core of tunes; the 30-odd issues of sacred music published in the colonies before *Urania* contained a total repertory of only 75 psalm-tunes. *Urania* almost doubled the size of the repertory: 69 of its 98 pieces were new to American printing. And *Urania*

destroyed once and for all the repertory's unity. The 1760s saw a dramatic increase in the repertory's size, from 75 psalm-tunes in 1760 to about 400 pieces by the end of the decade, including anthems, set-pieces, fuging-tunes, and ornate hymn-tunes. But, as in *Urania*, most of the new pieces were imported from England. When Billings's *New-England Psalm-Singer* appeared on the market with 126 new American pieces, it represented a tenfold increase in the number of American compositions printed. Thus Billings, who identified himself on the title-page of *The New-England Psalm-Singer* as a "native of Boston, in New-England," was the first self-declared American composer.

In view of the history of the dozen years following the publication of Billings's *New-England Psalm-Singer*, it might be expected that the American composer established himself as a presence in sacred music. In fact, that did happen. The Revolutionary War, waged from 1775 to 1781 and not formally concluded until the treaty of 1783, inhibited musical publication by creating unstable currency and shortages in paper and copper, from which the music was printed. Nevertheless, Billings himself brought out three more collections by the end of 1781, two of them entirely of his own music. And Andrew Law's *Select Harmony* (Cheshire, 1779) and Simeon Jocelin and Amos Doolittle's *Chorister's Companion* (New Haven, 1782) between them made available music by 15 previously unpublished American composers. The list includes Babcock, Brown, Oliver Brownson, Amos Bull, Bunnel, Asahel Carpenter, Amassa or Mark Antony Deaolph, Lewis Edson, Alexander Gillet, Ingersoll, Ichabod Johnson, Daniel Read, Joseph Strong, Benjamin West, and Abraham Wood. (Some of the first names are unknown.) Other hints of the American composer's emergence can be found: in the comment in 1773 by Daniel Bayley, a publisher who specialized in reprinting popular British tunebooks, that he expected "to procure some curious Pieces that are the Productions of America, by some masterly Hands, who have not yet permitted any of their Work to remain public;"[2] in Jocelin and Doolittle's index (1782), naming only "American Authors" of the tunes in the collection; and in evidence that tunes by American composers circulated widely in manuscript during these years before they found their way into print.[3]

Yet, for all these signs, no nationalistic rhetoric accompanied the American psalmodist's creative emergence. No one seems to have commented—at least not in print—on the swift transformation of the music of American psalmody from an imported to an Anglo-American repertory. The earliest historical statement on the process does not appear until 1786, in the *Worcester Collection* (Worcester), where Isaiah Thomas, the publisher, writes:

> For the progress of Psalmody in this country the Publick are in a great measure indebted to the musical abilities of Mr. *William Billings*, of Boston: It is but doing him justice here to observe,

that he was the first person we know of that attempted to compose Church Musick, in the New-England States; his musick has met with great approbation. . . . Several adepts in musick followed Mr. *Billings's* example, and the New-England states can now boast of many authors of Church Musick, whose compositions do them honour. (1st p.1., *verso*)

What Thomas says suggests that he saw the process as perfectly natural and inevitable. Had he attached real cultural significance to the advent of the native American composer, had he viewed it as an event of special nationalistic import, he might have been expected to comment further on it in later editions of the *Worcester Collection*. He did not.

After Billings's confessed reticence in 1770—a reticence he confirmed in his second collection, the *Singing Master's Assistant* (1778), by admitting to the public "that many pieces in [*The New-England Psalm-Singer*] were never worth my printing or your inspection" —the next two decades saw no further expressions of self-doubt from American composers. Billings's later tunebooks are free of apologies. Three more collections devoted to music by a single composer, besides Billings's appeared before 1790: Daniel Read's *American Singing Book* (New Haven, 1785), Jacob French's *New American Melody* (Boston, 1789), and Abraham Wood's *Divine Songs* (Boston, 1789). None contains any personal evaluative comment, nor do they give any sign that the composer-compilers believed that one was necessary. Moreover, compilers of eclectic collections in the 1780s said nothing in particular about their countrymen's increasing creative activity, nothing to suggest that they considered American psalmody inferior to or different from English. All indications are that as the repertory of psalmody grew in the 1770s and 1780s, both from new music composed by Americans and new music imported from Europe, Americans saw no particular import in the provenance of the music. Acculturation took place smoothly and silently.

That attitude changed dramatically in the next decade, as new composer-compilers came forward with collections of their own pieces. Isaiah Thomas, still located in Worcester, was now established in Boston as well, as senior partner of the publishing firm of Thomas and Andrews. Between 1791 and 1795 Thomas and Andrews brought out six collections of music by single composers. The apologies that appear in all except one are similar enough to suggest that apology was house policy. Samuel Holyoke (Harvard, class of 1789) was the first American since Billings to admit uncertainty about the quality of his music. Billings had pleaded youth; Holyoke, however, pled nationality. In the introduction to his *Harmonia Americana* (Boston, 1791), he wrote:

The advantages for studying the principles of harmony being, in this country, so limited, it cannot be expected that a composition of this nature can stand the test of criticism. (p. [4])

Oliver Holden, making his debut as a composer the next year, invoked Billings's earlier dictum that only the insistence of "friends" had induced him to publish his *American Harmony* (Boston, 1792). He added that he was

> conscious that, in point of composition, [the music] will not bear the test of criticism, especially with those whose advantages for acquiring the knowledge of so nice an art, have been greatly superior to those of the Author. (p. [2])

A slightly new twist on Holyoke's comment appeared at the head of *The Rural Harmony* (Boston, 1793), composed by Jacob Kimball (Harvard, class of 1780):

> In a country where music has not yet become a regular profession, it cannot be expected that a composition of this kind can stand a rigid criticism; but as every attempt to subserve the interest, or to encrease the innocent pleasures of the community, deserves public patronage, the author . . . without further apology, presents it to the public eye. (p. [ii])

Supply Belcher's *Harmony of Maine* (Boston, 1794) continues the litany:

> [The author] presents the following Work to the Public—not that he expects it would stand the test of rigid criticism; but as his design is to subserve the interest, and promote the innocent pleasures of the community, he hopes to meet the approbation and patronage of the candid judges of Musick. (p. [3])

Samuel Babcock in *The Middlesex Harmony* (1795) also throws himself upon the public mercy:

> [The author] after much solicitation . . . is induced to let the following Pieces appear in print. And although he is conscious of their imperfection, he still enjoys this consolation, that gentlemen whose musical abilities, as well as every other advantage, have been vastly superior to his, will not severely censure even what they cannot applaud. (p. [ii])

The sixth one-man work of the period, William Billings's *Continental Harmony*, was issued in 1794 by Thomas and Andrews at the behest of a committee organized to relieve the composer and his family's "distressed" financial condition. The introduction to the work shows Billings bumptious, unrepentant, and unapologetic. But an earlier subscription advertisement sent out by the publishers had assured the public that

> The Inspection and Revision of the whole is submitted by Mr. *Billings* to [a] committee, many of whom are deemed of approved knowledge in the science of Musick, and nothing will be offered to the publick but what they recommend and approve of.[4]

The expression of doubt about the quality of American music was not limited to composers discussing their own. It was taken up by compilers as well. Andrew Law, in *The Musical Primer* (Cheshire, 1793), was the first to accuse other Americans of compositional ineptness. In a characteristically uncompromising attack, Law denounced American composers for certain flaws which will be discussed below. Law's attack and the confessions of the psalmodists in the Thomas and Andrews stable were symptoms that the more innocent days of the 1780s were over, that American musicians were beginning to recognize differences between their music and the psalmody imported from Europe. As this recognition widened, it created a rhetorical etiquette for tunebook introductions. After 1790 hardly a single American composer published a collection of his own music without hat in hand. For example, James Newhall wrote in his *Vocal Harmony* (Northampton, 1803): "Critics in music are requested to behold errors in this work with an eye of candor, considering that imperfections in the works of a tyro are not phenomena" (p. [2]). Benjamin Holt warned in *The New-England Sacred Harmony* (Boston, 1803): "Should the scrutinizing connoisseur discover any defects in the ensuing work (as he probably may) he will remember that *error* is a characteristic of all human productions" (p. [2]). And there are many more examples that one could quote. One gets the impression that some musicians drew upon their ingenuity to make *their* amends something special. But some didn't bother. For example, in 1809 Hezekiah Moors of Mt. Holly, Vermont, headed his *Province Harmony* with the following:

> In a county where Musick has not yet become a regular calling, it cannot be expected that a Composition of this kind can stand an inflexible criticism. (p. [3])

And, reaching into his stock of eloquence, Joel Harmon of Pawlett, Vermont, headed his *Columbian Sacred Minstrel* in the same year with:

> It cannot be expected that a composition of this nature, (especially in a country where the advantages for studying music are so limited,) can stand the test of a rigid criticism. (p. [ii])

You will recognize the similarity of Moors's and Harmon's confessions, and you will also notice that they are taken virtually verbatim from the statements made by Holyoke and Kimball some years before. What this seems to demonstrate is that by around 1810 public apology was expected, and that American composers felt obliged to offer some form of self-deprecation—even if they had to borrow the words. In such an atmosphere a refusal to play the *mea culpa* game is rare. But there are examples. In the preface to his *Christian Harmony* (1805), Jeremiah Ingalls of Newbury, Vermont, wrote:

> Considering the multiplicity of apologies usually made, when productions of this nature are brought forward, the Author would inform the public that he has none to make. (p. [2])

Ingalls, however, was an exception. By around 1810, the only American composers who introduced new collections of their own music without an apology were those unaware of the established idea of the American composer of sacred music as an undertrained, bumbling novice. Thus, since Billings's time the idea of the American composer had been formulated, accepted—apparently with little hesitancy—and then, beginning in the 1790s, had taken on a decidedly self-patronizing taint.

Billings's second point in the introduction to *The New-England Psalm-Singer* concerns musical style—specifically the degree of musical elaboration found in psalmody. When he referred to the "modern Air and Manner of Singing," what he meant was the tendency in British psalmody beginning in the middle third of the 18th century to make increasing use of melismas, changes of texture, and points of imitation, as in the manner of the fuging-tune. Seventeenth and early 18th-century psalmody had been restricted essentially to unadorned tunes set in block chords. But English parish composers such as William Tans'ur, William Knapp, Joseph Stephenson, John Arnold, and Aaron Williams wrote in the new, more elaborate style. Their compositions formed much of the British repertory which between 1760 and the end of the Revolution was incorporated into American tunebooks. This new repertory overlaid the music carried down from the earliest American collections and, to some extent at least, served as a model for the American composers of the 1770s and 1780s.

Nineteenth-century historians of New England psalmody saw William Billings's primary contribution to be his introduction of a vibrant and secularized musical style into New England churches. Nahum Mitchell, himself a composer-compiler, wrote in 1841:

> Who can wonder that after an age of slow, dull, monotonous singing in our churches, confined at the same time to half a dozen thread bare tunes, our congregations should have been electrified and delighted with the chanting, song-like, spirited style which Billings introduced? [5]

As we can now see, the new style in colonial psalmody of the 1770s originated in England. But, obviously with the support of Billings, among others, it took root here quickly. By 1782, Simeon Jocelin was writing in the introduction to his *Chorister's Companion* of the profound musical changes he had observed:

> It is very obvious, that Psalmody hath undergone a considerable revolution, in most of our religious assemblies, within the course of a few years, not only with respect to the method and order of

singing, but even the tunes formerly in common use, are now generally laid aside, instead of which, those of a more lively and airy turn are substituted.

Jocelin did not look upon this turn of events as an unmixed blessing:

> Altho' many improvements have been made in Church Music, yet there appears a danger of erring, by introducing, in public worship, light and trifling airs, more becoming the theatre or shepherd's pipe; a liberty . . . by no means admissible in the solemnities of Divine Service. (p. [1])

Thus the issue was first stated. On the one hand there was, apparently, wide popular approval of the "modern Air and Manner of Singing" as a vitalizing musical, and perhaps religious, force. On the other, questions were beginning to arise about the appropriateness of certain kinds of music for sacred subjects. The issues raised in Jocelin's introduction were to become in the next three decades the focus for a major ideological controversy.

In the 1790s, the issue of stylistic appropriateness came to the forefront. Where earlier compilers had talked in generalities, criticisms now became specific. Samuel Holyoke, in the *Harmonia Americana* (1791), was the first to identify a particular species as devotionally unsuitable:

> Perhaps some may be disappointed, that fuging pieces are in general omitted. But the principal reason why few were inserted was the trifling effect produced by that sort of music; for the parts, falling in, one after another, conveying a different idea, confound the sense, and render the performance a mere jargon of words. (p. [4])

Holyoke's objection to text overlap in the fuging-tune, like his idea that American compositions could not withstand the test of "rigid criticism," was taken up by other compilers in succeeding years. Some, like Oliver Holden in *Plain Psalmody* (1800), called attention to their omission of fuging-tunes. Others acknowledged that the continuing public appetite for fuging-tunes made it hard not to include some, as Samuel Babcock admitted in *The Middlesex Harmony*, 2nd edition (1803):

> [The compiler] has not consulted his own inclination entirely in introducing fuging music into pieces intended for public worship: But as it has been the general practice, wherever he has given in to it, he has endeavoured to preserve the sense of the lines entire, so as not to 'make a jargon of words.' (p. [ii])

One gradually gets a sense that "fuging tune" and "fuging music" had become code words, implying not only imitation and text overlap but secularity, sprightliness, and a general elevation of senses over propriety in sacred music. Elias Mann's *Massachusetts Harmony* (1807) implied as much, as Mann sanctimoniously announced:

> In this Collection will be found none of those wild fugues, and rapid and confused movements, which have so long been the disgrace of congregational psalmody, and the contempt of the judicious and tasteful amateur. (p. [iii])

Fuging was, of course, only one element of the "Modern Air and Manner of Singing" that Billings had sought to emulate in his earliest compositions. Another aspect of the "modern" style was what Jocelin had described in 1782 as music of a "lively and airy turn."

In *The Union Harmony* (1793), Oliver Holden distinguished two general types of music and treated their merits as a matter of opinion:

> It has become a practice of late to introduce *new, airy* music into public worship, in preference to *grave* airs; the propriety, or impropriety of this depends, in some measure, upon the reception it meets with, among those who are far advanced in life, or have not the means of acquiring the knowledge of new tunes. In all worshipping societies, more or less of this description are found. In such cases, would it not be best to cultivate a spirit of accommodation, by adopting a number of tunes, both new and old, which are best calculated to express the various subjects to which they may occasionally be adapted, and at the same time give an opportunity to every one who wishes, to join in that part of worship which is equally the privilege and duty of all? (p. iv)

During the next decade Holden's flexibility on sacred style diminished considerably. In 1803, he declared in the introduction to *The Worcester Collection*, 8th edition:

> As sacred Poetry is generally best adapted to the plaintive, it is recommended to adopt that style in public worship, where rapid music is in use. Solemn airs . . . are always to be preferred to trifling, airy compositions, in devotional exercises; and will better accord with the sentiments and *feelings* of real worshippers. (p. [ii])

Holden's new sentiments accorded with those earlier expressed by Andrew Law in *The Art of Singing*, 2nd edition (1800):

> The man of piety and principle, of taste and discernment in music, and hence, indeed, all, who entertain a sense of decency and decorum in devotion, are oftentimes offended with that lifeless and insipid, or that frivolous and frolicksome succession and combination of sounds, so frequently introduced into churches, where all should be serious, animated and devout. . . . Much of the predominating Psalmody of this Country is more like song-singing, than like solemn praise. (p. [3]-4)

Thus a trend had been set in motion which ran counter to the practice established by Billings and his generation. The new notion was that one particular style was "suited to the solemnity of sacred devotion," as Oliver Holden put it in *The Charlestown Collection* (1803), p. [2]. And, as in *The Salem Collection of Classical Church Musick* (1805), collections began to appear in New England consisting mostly of European psalm-tunes from the pre-Tans'ur era. As William Cooper put it in the introduction to his *Beauties of Church Music* (1804), "It has become a general opinion among good singers, that the music in use before the revolution in 1775, is much better than that which has succeeded" (p. [iii]). The anonymous compiler of *The Salem Collection* linked musical taste with religion in his justification for returning to ancient psalmody. "Most of our modern psalmody," he wrote, "is not less offensive to a correct musical taste, than it is disgusting to the sincere friends of publick devotion" (p. [iii]). Thus, under the spell of pious ideology, American psalmody in New England was by the first decade of the 19th century returning to the repertory it had had before the infusion of new British and American music in the 1760s, '70s, and '80s.

In *The New-England Psalm-Singer*, Billings had raised a third issue, the question of musical idiom and the supposed flaws of his own. The consciousness of these flaws was responsible for much of the self-deprecation shown by American psalmodists of the 1790s and later. And it is interesting to watch the evolution of attitudes toward these flaws.

In order to understand precisely where American composers felt deficient, it is necessary to say a few words about their idea of music theory. American psalmodists of the 18th century, unlike almost all of their European contemporaries, lacked training and skill at the keyboard. Their medium was the four-voice chorus, not the organ, harpsichord, or piano. The few comments that they left about their technique of composition suggest that they composed successively rather than simultaneously, first writing a melody, next setting a bass to it, then adding treble and counter parts in turn. Virtually all they ever say about the "rules" of composition suggests that "rules" to them meant a knowledge of intervals as consonant or dissonant and a knowledge that voice-independence was a goal of part-writing. What eluded most of them, at least before the turn of the century, was the horizontal dimension of harmony, the chord-connections which underlay virtually all European music of the period. Almost all 18th-century American sacred music is set to poetry. That helps to mask its harmonic irregularities, for the musical phrases are shaped by the textual meter, and the resulting melodic symmetries help to generate harmonic formulas which operate as one might expect in European music. But a smooth flow toward clear harmonic destinations, inherent in thoroughbass practice, is missing from most

New England psalmody. The introduction of organs into churches helped to sound the death knell of the New England musical idiom.

As noted before, it was not until the 1790s that American composers began to admit publicly that their music was different from European. The differences were quickly located in the harmonic dimension—as pointed out by Holyoke's statement quoted earlier. Andrew Law's attack on American composers in *The Musical Primer* (1793) was based chiefly on a harmonic complaint:

> A considerable part of American composition is in reality faulty. It consists more of the sweet and perfect cords, than European music, which aims at variety and energy, by introducing the perfect cords less frequently.

Law correctly noticed the American composer's fondness for incomplete triads or open fifths—a trait which, by the way, would be uncharacteristic of any music with keyboard accompaniment, or of any music written from a thoroughbass background, since thoroughbass takes the triad as its elemental unit. Whether the modern ear would agree that the result of open fifths in profusion is "languid and lifeless," as Law wrote elsewhere, while the European penchant for filling in all triads shows "variety and energy," is another matter. Jacob Kimball was writing as a practicing composer, not a judge, when he mentioned harmony in the introduction to his *Rural Harmony* (1793):

> [The compiler] has aimed at originality in his compositions, and endeavoured to deviate . . . from the common style; where he has given into it, he has attempted to improve it by a particular attention to the harmony. (p. [ii])

Apparently at pains to separate himself from his harmonically inept countrymen, Kimball harmonized his music with a vocabulary approaching that of the orthodox European idiom.

A key work in American psalmody was published by Thomas and Andrews in 1795: Hans Gram, Oliver Holden, and Samuel Holyoke's *Massachusetts Compiler of Theoretical and Practical Elements of Sacred Vocal Music. The Massachusetts Compiler* begins with a 36-page introduction, extracted from various European thoroughbass treatises, which offered for the first time in the United States a full explanation of the principles of 18th-century functional harmony. Apparently the brainchild of Gram, a Danish immigrant and organist of the Brattle Street Church in Boston, *The Massachusetts Compiler* was a milestone in the field, and it was frequently cited in later years by advocates of European musical style. *The Massachusetts Compiler*, with its introductory treatise and its music "chiefly selected or adapted from modern European publications," provided the American composer with approved new models for composition. But compilers were not anxious to discard the whole familiar repertory in the name of correctness. William Cooper explained the compiler's dilemma in the preface to his *Beauties of Church Music* of 1804:

> Our present collections contain a medley of good and bad tunes, in continual contradiction to each other in point of composition. . . . The Compiler, in this collection . . . has been under the necessity of either excluding some pieces of music which he highly esteems, or to make some little alterations in the harmony. He has preferred the latter. (p. [iii])

Other compilers followed Cooper's practice of printing favorite American tunes with touched-up harmonies. In fact, Daniel Read, one of the few composers who underwent the process of musical conversion and public repentance, "corrected" the harmonies of several of his own pieces for *The New Haven Collection* (1818), and so the pieces are labelled. And, as the compilers of *The Salem Collection* (1805) pointed out, the harmonic deficiencies of American compilers had affected even the archaic repertory they were making available:

> The tunes here given to the publick may perhaps be found in the different compilations already made, yet they are . . . deeply buried under the crudities of half-learned harmonists. (p. iv)

Thus, recognition that Europeans and Americans practiced different harmonic principles led in the early 19th century to a reharmonizing of much of the repertory, and to the addition of figured bass to many collections. One goal of the process was to remove or to conceal diversity. The repertory had grown infinitely larger than it had been, of course, in the days before Billings. But the impulse set in motion in the 1790s was to homogenize, to dissolve in a normalized harmonic language, the marked individuality of the various kinds of music that Americans had chosen to sing in praise of God.

So far, I have tried to isolate three issues important in American psalmody, and to show that a similar process of crystallization, of hardening, took place in all three. The notion of the American as an ill-trained composer of trifling sacred pieces filled with musical solecisms was a creation of the 1790s. A process of musical reform set out in the 1790s to purge the tradition of these elements. By around 1810 tunebooks published in the larger American cities carried a repertory heavily weighted toward European tunes, or Europeanized American tunes. Thus, from the perspective of musical repertory, American psalmody evolved from almost exclusively European music before 1760 to a truly Anglo-American repertory around 1790, and back toward the earlier European music by about 1810. That process cannot help but raise nationalistic hackles. Yet, the primary issue is not musical nationalism. It is the arbitrary and unnatural character of the process itself.

Between 1760 and 1790 American psalmody developed essentially free of ideology. The rapid increase in the diversity, as well as the size, of the repertory during those years is evidence enough that no special ideological criteria shaped it. In fact, the repertory in the period depended chiefly upon the personal preferences of individual tunebook compilers. And if there was any predominant preference it was for eclecticism. Compilers like Andrew Law and Simeon Jocelin, in the last years of the American Revolution, issued compilations in which 16th- and 17th-century Genevan and British psalm-tunes, music of the 18th-century English parish tradition, florid hymn-tunes modelled on the style of the mid-century London stage, and tunes by their Massachusetts and Connecticut neighbors were all mixed together under the only umbrella that could possibly cover them: "favorite pieces." And this kind of mixture proved to be commercially successful. The best sellers among 18th- and early 19th-century American tunebooks were Isaiah Thomas's *Worcester Collection*, (eight editions), the anonymous *Federal Harmony* (Boston; six editions), Andrew Adgate's *Philadelphia Harmony* (Philadelphia; nine editions); *Village Harmony* (Exeter; seventeen editions), and Little & Smith's *Easy Instructor* (Philadelphia and Albany; more than forty printings). All displayed what William Cooper had called "continual contradiction to each other in point of composition." Dominated by a spirit of inclusiveness, American psalmody from 1760 to 1790 can be seen as a single, burgeoning mainstream practice.

In the 1790s, for the first time since the bitter early 18th-century controversies over Regular Singing and hymn-singing, American psalmody was penetrated by ideas—ideas about the American as a composer, about musical style, about musical grammar. Once formulated and expressed, these ideas immediately gained currency among people to whom ideas were more important than musical experience. The notions that American composers, inexperienced and handicapped by the thinness of their country's musical life, were less skillful composers than Europeans and that worship was a solemn business requiring dignified, restrained music were plausible and acceptable as ideas. And these ideas came to have a powerful influence—especially among the educated and the "Establishment"—upon the tradition in the early years of the 19th century. They fragmented what had been a mainstream. Compilers turned increasingly to the ancient tunes as the heart of the repertory they printed. Composers reacted differently depending upon their circumstances. Those in outlying areas of northern New England, upper New York State, and western Pennsylvania ignored or were unaware of the new ideology and continued to write in their native, untutored idiom. (This stream went southward through the Shenandoah Valley of Virginia and westward along the Ohio River to establish itself as a flourishing rural shape-note practice by the 1820s.) Others—Holyoke, Holden, and Kimball among them—studied European musical techniques and tried to match the florid style of later 18th-century English hymnodists like Martin Madan and Samuel Arnold. Ultimately the most influential track was taken by composers such as Lowell Mason and Thomas Hastings, who in the 1820s set themselves to writing the simple, harmonically chaste, "devotional" style of tune, actually a modern evocation of the plain psalmody of 17th-century Great Britain. The Mason-Hastings idiom set the tone for urban American hymnody through the Civil War. The ideas we have mentioned transformed the repertory which survived in urban New England and in the larger eastern cities. The musical complexity and appeal to the senses of "fuging" was rejected. The involvement of a whole congregation in unaccompanied polyphony gave way to a hard-and-fast division between congregational and choir music, with the congregation restricted to simple tunes of narrow vocal range, and with all music-making supported by an organ. What had been a single mainstream practice was transformed by ideas into a set of categories.

I have described American psalmody of the period from 1760 to 1790 as a "practice," which the *Oxford English Dictionary* defines as a "habitual carrying on of something . . . action as distinguished from profession, theory, knowledge." Psalmody as a practice was not entirely devoid of ideas. But practitioners' ideas stem from their experience, not from their capacity to speculate and to reason. Their ideas are specific rather than general, for practitioners occupy the same framework as the thing they practice; they have not separated the practice from themselves and their practice of it. They are not curious about its totality, only about its details. If a practice works from inside toward the outside, a category works the opposite way. Immanuel Kant's use of the terms in philosophy captures this fact deftly. For Kant, category means "the pure *a priori* conceptions of the understanding, which the mind applies (as forms or frames) to the matter of knowledge received from *sense*, in order to raise it into an *intelligible* notion or object of knowledge."[6] The category is a device by which the mind organizes experience. It is a "form" or a "frame" by which sense experience is made "intelligible." It imposes order by bringing experience under its control.

American psalmody was a practice that was thought to "mean" nothing in particular until the 1790s, when the intellectual frame described above was introduced. From that time on, psalmody became a category, or a set of categories, developing within that frame.

A category fosters a relationship between sense and intellect, or heart and brain, very different from the relationship found in a practice. In a practice the senses are dominant, and the

intellect functions in matters of detail. Conception is taken care of—carried on, as the
O.E.D.'s definition goes—more or less habitually. A practice is conservative; its limits,
though mostly unspoken, are deeply felt and rather narrow, and anything accepted into
an artistic practice is accepted on its own merits as viewed by the practitioners. It is for-
eign to the nature of a practice to admit anything for external reasons. Thus, the artistic
standard of a practice is rooted chiefly in the senses of the practitioners. A category op-
erates quite differently. It may originally be rooted in the senses, but once it reaches the
level of the intellect and becomes an "intelligible notion" (in Kant's phrase) it gains a
life of its own and can go its own way with no particular connection to the sense experience which created it in the first place. This is very different from a musical practice,
in which the participants *have* no ideas detachable from their day-to-day musical activity.
Musical categories can be dangerous precisely because they depend upon ideas *about* music
rather than upon music. As the decade of the 1790s shows, the ideas which defined psalmody as a category became standard rhetorical figures and gathered a momentum of their
own, detached from the experience of music.

To ring in our title here, a musical practice is a vernacular—a kind of music that H. Wiley
Hitchcock describes in his *Music in the United States* as "plebian, native, not approached
self-consciously but simply grown into as one grows into one's vernacular tongue; music
understood and appreciated simply for its utilitarian or entertainment value." Hitchcock's
opposite number for vernacular is "cultivated"—a body of music," he explains, "that America had to cultivate consciously, music faintly exotic, to be approached with some effort,
and to be appreciated for its edification, its moral, spiritual or aesthetic values."[7]
Hitchcock's insight is very fruitful. For while it describes two kinds of music, it also identifies two different attitudes toward music. "Vernacular" and "cultivated" are not just
descriptions of the character of objects; they describe ways of approaching the objects.
Thus, for example, Cecil Sharp's searching for English folksongs in the Appalachians early
in this century, though concentrated on a vernacular tradition, was conducted in a cultivated spirit; Sharp was looking for art—for music "appreciated for its edification, its moral,
spiritual or aesthetic value." Conversely, when Beethoven's "Moonlight" Sonata finds its
way into the canon of Muzak, or into a football half-time show, it can no longer be approached "for its edification, its moral, spiritual or aesthetic values." It has become utilitarian and vernacular.

When I began to frame this topic I thought that at this point in the lecture I would be able
to plug my "practice" and "category" distinction into the "vernacular" and "cultivated"
framework, equate the one with vitality and the other with decadence, and be done with it.

Psalmody before 1790 was clearly a practice and a vernacular tradition, and it was turned into something else. Ideas transformed a freely-chosen, heterogeneous practice into a self-conscious, increasingly homogeneous category. However, the outcome of this hardening from vernacular to something else produced a very different result from what I think we mean, or should mean, when we say "cultivated." By removing from the repertory the music which did not conform to the standard set by the category they had established, the most extreme reformers took their stand with pre-1760 British psalmody. Thus, the creative contributions of the last half of the 18th century were swept away as if they had never existed. Psalmodists, once participants in and contributors to a flourishing practice, became guardians of a fixed taste—a category. Psalmody had recast itself in a new, uncompromising image; it had become not cultivated but reactionary.

NOTES

1. My preface to the facsimile reprint of *Urania* (New York: Da Capo Press, 1974) identifies many of the musical sources upon which Lyon drew and describes the influence of this important collection.

2. Daniel Bayley, *The New Universal Harmony* (Newburyport: the author, 1773), 1st p. 1., *verso*.

3. See Richard Crawford and David P. McKay, "Music in Manuscript: A Massachusetts Tune-book of 1782," *Proceedings of the American Antiquarian Society*, Vol. 84, Pt. 1 (April, 1974).

4. *Massachusetts Magazine* (August, 1792), printed on endpapers. Also quoted in Henry M. Brooks, *Olden-Time Music* (Boston: Ticknor, 1888), p. 265.

5. [Nahum Mitchell,] "William Billings," *The Musical Reporter* (July, 1841), p. 301.

6. Quoted from the *Oxford English Dictionary* (1933 ed.), Vol. II, p. 181.

7. H. Wiley Hitchcock, *Music in the United States,* 2nd ed. (Englewood Cliffs: Prentice-Hall, 1974), p. 51.

MUSICAL PUBLICATIONS QUOTED

Babcock, Samuel. *The Middlesex Harmony*. Boston: Thomas and Andrews, 1795.
_____._____, 2nd ed. Boston: Thomas and Andrews, 1803.

Belcher, Supply. *The Harmony of Maine*. Boston: Thomas and Andrews, 1794.

Billings, William. *The New-England Psalm-Singer*. Boston: Edes and Gill, 1770.

Cooper, William. *The Beauties of Church Music*. Boston: Manning & Loring, [1804].

Harmon, Joel Jr. *The Columbian Sacred Minstrel*. Northampton: A. Wright, 1809.

Holden, Oliver. *American Harmony*. Boston: Thomas and Andrews, 1792.

_____. *The Charlestown Collection*. Boston: Thomas and Andrews, 1803.

[_____] *Plain Psalmody*. Boston: Thomas and Andrews, 1800.

_____. *The Union Harmony*, Vol. I. Boston: Thomas and Andrews, 1793.

_____. *The Worcester Collection*, 8th ed. Boston: Thomas and Andrews, 1803.

Holt, Benjamin Jr. *The New-England Sacred Harmony*. Boston: Thomas and Andrews,

Holyoke, Samuel. *Harmonia Americana*. Boston: Thomas and Andrews, 1791.

Ingalls, Jeremiah. *The Christian Harmony*. Exeter: Henry Ranlet, 1805.

[Jocelin, Simeon, and Amos Doolittle.] *The Chorister's Companion*. New Haven: for
    Jocelin and Doolittle, 1782.

Kimball, Jacob. *The Rural Harmony*. Boston: Thomas and Andrews, 1793.

Law, Andrew. *The Musical Primer*. Cheshire: William Law, 1793.

_____. *The Art of Singing*, 3rd [*recte* 2nd] ed. Cheshire: [Samuel Andrews], 1800.

Mann, Elias. *The Massachusetts Collection*. Boston: Manning and Loring, 1807.

Moors, Hezekiah. *The Province Harmony*. Boston: J.T. Buckingham, 1809.

Newhall, James. *The Vocal Harmony*. Northampton: Andrew Wright, 1803.

The Salem Collection. Salem: Joshua Cushing, 1805.

The Worcester Collection. Worcester: Isaiah Thomas, 1786.

The Institute for Studies in American Music at Brooklyn College, established in 1971, is a division of the Department of Music in the college's School of the Performing Arts. The Institute contributes to the field of American-music studies by publishing a monograph series, bibliographies, and a newsletter. It encourages and supports research by sponsoring fellowships for distinguished scholars and participating in conferences and symposia dealing with all areas of American music, including art music, popular music, and folk music. I.S.A.M. activities include concerts held at Brooklyn College for students, faculty, and the public. In addition to serving as an information center, the Institute cooperates with other institutions devoted to American-music projects. It co-sponsored (with Yale University) the 1974 Charles Ives Centennial Festival-Conference and is currently supervising the series, Recent Researches in American Music, published by A-R Editions.